MANY CONSERVATIVES, perhaps a majority, now believe that the Common Core State Standards are one of the worst things to ever happen to American education. And why wouldn't they believe it? For the past three years, people have been bombarded by conservative media outlets and think tanks with scary-sounding allegations that the Obama administration illegally imposed the Common Core on the states and that the president's power grab is leading to a dumbed-down, leftist curriculum in the schools.

Here are just a few of the urban legends spun by anti-Common Core writers and activists, followed by an actual fact or two:

➤ President Obama is using the Common Core to "move the country's education system toward a federally controlled curriculum," says Stanley Kurtz, a leading conservative author. Moreover, according to Kurtz, the president's old friend from the West Side of Chicago, 1960s Weather Underground terrorist William Ayers was among those behind the federal plot. Another conservative education writer, Mary Grabar, claims that "the Ayers educational brand or philosophy is all over Common Core."

Fact: The Common Core is not a curriculum. In any event, Ayers and his leftist education comrades vehemently oppose the standards.

➤ In December 2012, this headline appeared above a *Daily Telegraph* story about the Common Core: "Schools in America are to drop classic books such as Harper Lee's *To Kill a Mockingbird* and J. D. Salinger's *Catcher in the Rye* from their curriculum in favour of 'informational texts.'" According to the article's anonymous author, "American literature classics are to be replaced by insulation manuals and plant inventories in US classrooms by 2014." Despite its lack of a single source, the article was republished by the Drudge Report and then went viral on conservative media.

Fact: The Common Core doesn't rule out any of these works of fiction, or indeed any literary classic.

➤ A paper published by a leading conservative think tank charges that the Obama administration knowingly violated federal statutes and the U.S. Constitution by imposing the Common Core Standards and their associated curricula on the states.

Fact: There is no federal imposition. States are completely free to say no thank you to the federal government, and seven have already done so. The claim of illegality is nothing more than a lawyer's argument, unsupported by a single judicial authority.

Many of the purported "exposés" of the Common Core are hardly worth rebutting. Still, just to give readers a sense of the bizarro, here's an excerpt from one screed titled

Opposition to Common Core by the Tea Party and other activist groups has the feel of a populist revolt.

"Common Core Pornography," published by Pajamas Media: "Common Core reading materials are designed to 'groom' young people and leave them vulnerable to molestation and sexual abuse."

It's understandable that conservatives who believe such tall tales would want to see the education initiative they now call "Obamacore" rolled back. Opposition to Common Core by the Tea Party and other activist groups has the feel of a populist revolt. It has already succeeded in pressuring many Republican candidates and elected officials to reject the standards. Indiana and Oklahoma have withdrawn from the Common Core, and the program is in peril in several other states.

Most recently, Governor Scott Walker of Wisconsin called on his state's legislature to dump Common Core and replace it "with standards set by the people of Wisconsin." Bobby Jindal, Louisiana's governor and a Republican presidential candidate, was for the Common Core before he was against it, apparently because he suddenly discovered it was all part of an Obama plot. All this is a sure sign that support for Common Core has become toxic for Republican candidates in the 2016 presidential primaries.

Conservatives should be careful what they wish for. They could find themselves being held responsible for undermining the only education reform of the past 40 years that has any chance of restoring traditional academic content to the classroom. They might also be remembered for using the big-lie technique and for smearing prominent conservatives who support the Common Core. Chester E. Finn, president of the Thomas B. Fordham Institute and a supporter of national education standards for the past 25 years, is regularly denounced by activists for "doing it for the money" – i.e., accepting a grant from the Bill & Melinda Gates Foundation to support Fordham's work on national standards. One anti-Common Core writer even referred to Finn as "Baghdad Bob," recalling Saddam Hussein's propaganda minister.

If the Common Core fails (and it might), we will not soon discover better alternatives for public schools, as conservative activists imagine. Rather, Americans will remain stuck with the vast wasteland of a public-education system bereft of serious academic standards and a coherent curriculum. The nation's K-12 schools will then continue turning out what Emory University Professor Mark Bauerlein has called "the dumbest generation." (That's the title of Bauerlein's excellent 2008 book on the failure of the public schools to prepare young people for college-level work.)

One other likely result of Common Core failure is that the progressive education movement, which has already inflicted great damage on schools, will retain its pervasive influence on what is taught (or, rather, not taught) in America's classrooms. Conservatives who help bring down the Common Core will thus have given an unexpected gift to the education left. Ironically, most leftists also oppose the Common Core, but at least they're smart enough to know that if the Common Core crashes, progressive education ideology will still rule the classroom.

Regardless of whether one believes that the main threat to the Common Core Standards emanates from the left or the right, its demise will harm the country's schools. As a conservative, I remain convinced that, faults and all, the Common Core still presents a golden opportunity and a challenge for states and school districts to rethink what is taught in their classrooms. The standards are more than just a list of learning objectives and skills that American students are expected to achieve by the end of each grade level. The most hopeful part of the new standards is that they reject the instructional malpractice that prevents public schools from fulfilling their historic mission of producing literate American citizens who know something about their country's history and its republican heritage. Contrary to the conservatives' complaints, the Common Core is, in fact, a document that the founders would approve.

The Common Core is not a curriculum, as many critics have falsely claimed. But it emphatically calls for states and school districts to implement the standards with "a well-developed, content-rich curriculum." Because of that instructional guideline, there is now at least the possibility of a serious discussion in the schools about the role of academic content knowledge and a coherent curriculum in raising student achievement.

That's a conversation that hasn't taken place in American education for almost half a century. It also means long-overdue recognition for the prophetic warnings issued a quarter-century ago about the calamities of progressive education by E. D. Hirsch Jr., one of America's greatest education thinkers and also one of its most neglected. Proper implementation of the Common Core will bring attention and support for Hirsch's Core Knowledge curriculum (it already has in a few states), which is perfectly aligned with the standards and has been proven to raise the academic performance of poor children.

Instead of trying to pull down this entire edifice, still full of promise, conservative education activists ought to be exploring ways to exploit the openings provided by the new standards to restore a coherent, knowledge-based curriculum to the public schools. That's a reform worth fighting for on behalf of all American children.

II

To appreciate what is now at stake for public education, it's worth looking at the performance of our K-12 schools on the eve of the Common Core rollout in 2012. A vivid snapshot was provided by the National Assessment of Educational Progress (NAEP), also called the Nation's Report Card. NAEP is a federally funded, independent testing agency that periodically measures the education achievement of American students.

Perhaps the most significant of NAEP's many grade-level assessments are the reading tests that, beginning in 1971, have been administered every four years to a representative national sample of 17-year-olds. That's because the level of reading proficiency of children who have completed nearly 13 years of schooling is, arguably, the best measure of the success (or lack of success) of the nation's public schools. Math is very important, of course, but verbal ability is the essential tool for college readiness and also closely predicts future economic success. As Professor Hirsch has noted, "The achievement of high universal literacy is the key to all other fundamental improvements in American education."

That's why the results of the 2012 NAEP reading tests for 17-year-olds on the most recent assessment was such a dispiriting commentary on the condition of the schools. The tests confirmed that there had been no improvement in reading for 11th- and 12th-graders since the first national tests were administered in 1971. NAEP assessments of 17-year-olds in civics and U.S. history similarly exposed the amazingly low level of general knowledge by college-bound students.

If the Common Core fails (and it might), we will not soon discover better alternatives for public schools, as conservative activists imagine.

(On one of the tests, only 43 percent of 17-year-olds correctly identified the half-century in which the Civil War was fought.)

Throughout the past 40 years of education stagnation, there was no shortage of high-level study groups aimed at turning around the schools. In 1983, President Ronald Reagan's education secretary, Terrel Bell, established a national commission to study the precipitous decline in American students' SAT scores and their poor performance on international assessments. The bipartisan panel's report, titled *A Nation at Risk,* began with these ominous and now memorable words: "The educational foundations of our society are presently being eroded by a rising tide of mediocrity that threatens our very future as a Nation and a people." Among the report's laundry list of recommendations for improving U.S. education: raising standards, creating a core curriculum for students, higher salaries for teachers, and a longer school day.

SAT scores and NAEP reading assessments hardly moved over the next 30 years, but it was not for a lack of trying. States, local school districts, and the federal government periodically announced new reform initiatives, each based on a unique theory about the causes of the nation's poor education performance.

For example, in response to claims by liberal advocates that public schools – particularly those enrolling a high percentage of poor children – lacked sufficient financial resources, total spending on U.S. K-12 education went up enormously and is now the highest in the world on a per capita basis.

Conservative education reformers argued instead that the best therapy for the public schools was market competition and school choice. This led to an expansion of charter schools and voucher programs.

Reflecting the views of school reformers who bemoaned our education system's lack of accountability for students and teachers, the 2002 No Child Left Behind (NCLB) law mandated a greatly expanded testing regime in the states, along with tough federal sanctions for schools who failed to meet new performance standards. Unfortunately, none of these "system" reforms led to any substantial improvement in academic performance, as shown by the dismal 2012 NAEP reading results for 17-year-olds and the continuing stagnant SAT scores of American high school seniors.

Nevertheless, one necessary reform was

never tried at the state or federal levels during the four decades of education failure. It was the curriculum, stupid. Indeed, in the schools of education where the nation's future teachers were trained, the prevailing wisdom continued to be that there was no need for schools to follow a sequenced, grade-by-grade curriculum or even impart a coherent body of content knowledge to students.

Throughout this period, the schools remained under the sway of the progressive education movement that by the 1960s had dominated American education. Instead of teaching young children to read by using the proven method of explicit phonics instruction, progressive educators supported a teaching philosophy known as "whole language" (later called "balanced literacy"). Instead of teaching "mere" facts, teachers encouraged students to "construct" their own knowledge. Progressives followed a "child centered" instructional model based on the assumption that all children were natural readers and writers. Thus, with the right classroom environment and a helping hand from teachers, children could be inspired to find their individual paths to literacy.

Hirsch, then a professor of English at the University of Virginia and one of America's leading literary critics, was able to connect the dots between the ascendancy of progressive education doctrines and the decline in the reading ability of the nation's schoolchildren. In his best-selling 1987 book, *Cultural Literacy*, Hirsch declared, "The unacceptable failure of our schools has occurred not because our teachers are inept but chiefly because they are compelled to teach a fragmented curriculum based on faulty education theories."

The disappearance of a coherent American curriculum didn't occur by chance, Hirsch insisted. Rather, it was intended, quite deliberately, by the ed schools. It wasn't that education professors favored the wrong curriculum but that they stood for no curriculum at all. Citing Romantic theories of child development dating back to Jean-Jacques Rousseau and more recently to the educational theories of John Dewey, progressive educators assured the public that with just some assistance from teachers, children would figure it out as they went along. In their view, American children certainly didn't need a constricting and "developmentally inappropriate" curriculum stressing the historical deeds of dead white males.

Cultural Literacy became a surprise national best seller in part because it appealed to parents who were beginning to notice the lack of academic rigor in their children's classrooms. Hirsch also showed that the most devastating consequence of educational progressivism was that it widened, rather than narrowed, the gap in intellectual capital between middle-class children and those from disadvantaged families.

"Learning builds cumulatively on learning," Hirsch wrote. "By encouraging an early education that is free of 'unnatural' bookish knowledge and of 'inappropriate' pressure to exert hard effort, [progressive education] virtually ensures that children from well-educated homes who happen to be primed with academically relevant background knowledge which they bring with them to school, will learn faster than disadvantaged children who do not bring such knowledge with them and do not receive it at school." This essential background knowledge could only be provided through a planned, coherent curriculum. Without that curriculum, disadvantaged children inevitably fall even further behind, particularly in reading.

According to Hirsch, well-meaning school reformers merely advocating structural reforms – i.e., charters, vouchers, and accountability schemes for teachers – ignored the most potent force for academic achievement. The classroom was the "primal scene" of all education improvement, Hirsch noted. "The effort to develop a standard sequence of core knowledge is, to put it bluntly, absolutely essential to effective educational reform in the United States."

Although Hirsch's theories were backed by consensus research findings in cognitive

> *Throughout the past 40 years of education stagnation, there was no shortage of high-level study groups aimed at turning around the schools.*

science and psycholinguistics about how children learn to read, the ed school professoriate was not about to accept interference from a meddlesome outsider criticizing their pet progressive theories. With the notable exception of teachers-union leader Albert Shanker, the leftist education establishment turned on Hirsch, branding him as a reactionary, an elitist, and a defender of white privilege – all for proposing that America's public schools offer children the academic content they desperately needed to become proficient readers and knowledgeable citizens. Hirsch's books calling for a coherent, grade-by-grade curriculum and the teaching of content knowledge were virtually banned by the schools of education. Instead, the most popular course text in the schools of education remained *Pedagogy of the Oppressed*, by the Brazilian Marxist Paulo Freire. (More than a million copies have been sold to date.) Freire urged future teachers to turn their classrooms into centers of opposition to the prevailing capitalist order.

By political persuasion, Hirsch is a liberal Democrat. Nevertheless, his call for a Core Knowledge curriculum received crucial support from prominent conservative reformers, including former U.S. Education Secretary William Bennett; the Fordham Institute's Chester E. Finn; and the noted education historian Diane Ravitch (though she's now a leftist and opposes the Common Core). Finn and Ravitch served in President George H. W. Bush's Education Department, where they used the administration's bully pulpit to advance the cause of national standards.

President George W. Bush's education

agenda emphasized the accountability reforms written into NCLB. Nevertheless, Finn and Ravitch continued to build support within school-reform circles for national standards and Hirsh's Core Knowledge curriculum. Ravitch wrote a monograph for the prestigious Brookings Institution on the case for national education standards. In 2005 she published an influential op-ed piece in the *New York Times* bemoaning the current low level of academic performance of American students. "Our fourth-grade students generally do well when compared with their peers in other nations, but eighth-grade students are only average globally, and 12th graders score near the bottom in comparison with students in many European and Asian nations," Ravitch wrote. She also criticized President Bush for abandoning the previous Bush and Clinton administrations' push for national standards and, instead, pursuing a strategy of "50 states, 50 standards, 50 tests." "The evidence is growing that this approach has not improved student achievement," Ravitch wrote. "Americans must recognize that we need national standards, national tests and a national curriculum."

By the standard of today's Common Core debates, Ravitch's call for not only national standards and national tests but also a national curriculum may seem radical, even utopian. Yet many education reformers in the nation's capital, particularly conservatives, supported her ideas. Ravitch's *Times* op-ed was part of the Fordham Institute's effort to revive the standards movement and to institute curriculum reforms inspired by Hirsch's core knowledge approach. (Ravitch was then a member of the boards of the Fordham Institute and the Core Knowledge Foundation.)

In 2006, Fordham published a widely disseminated report renewing the call for national standards and national tests. "For the first time in almost a decade, people are seriously weighing the value of instituting national standards and tests in American K-12 education," the report stated. It also included the response of various education experts, including several prominent conservatives, to the question of "how a system of national standards and tests might be designed."

Nevertheless, the standards movement still faced a daunting problem: there seemed to be no clear pathway through the thicket of national and legislative politics leading to the drafting of an acceptable set of standards that might be embraced by 50 states (or at least most of them). Nor was it even clear who might write the standards document.

As it turned out, two Washington, D.C.-based organizations, the National Governors Association and the Council of Chief State School Officers (representing 50 state education chiefs) stepped into the breach. The College Board and ACT soon joined the effort. Leaders of these diverse education groups declared that after decades of unproductive philosophical debates, it was time to act. They assembled a consortium of education experts and recruited writers to draft a coherent set of national standards in English Language Arts and Mathematics for grades K-12.

III

As this historical overview suggests, long before the official Common Core documents were released in 2010, there was a serious bipartisan campaign to bring about some form of national education standards. The standards movement traced its roots back to the publication of the *Nation at Risk* report in 1983. Moreover, prominent education conservatives played a leading role in advancing this particular reform over the next several decades. Contrary to the claims of critics on the right, the Common Core Standards did not rise like a phoenix out of the Obama administration. And contrary to the claims of the education left, the Common Core was not created and then imposed on the schools because Bill Gates bribed the nation's key education players with hundreds of millions of dollars in foundation grants.

It is true that the combination of federal grants to the states, plus Gates Foundation funding, played an important role in pushing the Common Core from just one more education reform proposal to the early stage of implementation in the states (45 at first and now down to 43). The critics are at least right about that. Yet this financial support also made the Common Core vulnerable to demagogic attacks from education activists of the left and right.

I have described some of the canards about the Common Core Standards concocted by conservatives. It's equally worth noting that for many leftist critics of the standards, billionaire philanthropist Gates plays the role of deus ex machina stealing American public education. According to the progressive education activist Paul Horton, Common Core is "the product of a push by private foundations acting in the interest of multinational corporations to colonize public education in the United States and in other areas projected to be developed as core production and assembly areas in the emerging global economy."

It is hard to say which claim is more absurd on its face – the right-wing activists' assertion that the Common Core is President Obama's instrument for "federalizing the schools," or the leftist education activists' claim that the Common Core is Bill Gates's vehicle for privatizing the schools and "colonizing public education." Conservative and leftist critiques of Common Core now often overlap into one unified conspiracy theory, featuring lurid allegations of a plot to bypass the hallowed

---

One necessary reform was never tried at the state or federal levels during the four decades of education failure. It was the curriculum, stupid.

American principle of local control of the schools.

Notwithstanding three years of misinformation on this issue, the plain fact is that the process of creating the Common Core Standards and then persuading states to adopt it has been entirely consistent with the historical traditions of American federalism. The standards were written by private, nongovernmental organizations and urged on the states with the sweetener of federal grants. Yet all the states were free to decline the Common Core and stick with their old standards without any penalty other than not qualifying for a relatively small amount of additional federal money. The feds not only haven't interfered with the curriculum decisions made by the states as part of their Common Core adoptions, but they haven't even expressed any curricular preferences.

By contrast, President George W. Bush's NCLB reforms were draconian in enforcing new federal education policies on the states and localities. Under the threat of losing their annual federal Title I funding for high-poverty schools, all states were forced by NCLB regulations to begin testing students annually in math and reading in third through eighth grades. NCLB was an unprecedented, federally imposed expansion of the testing regime. (And it looks more and more unwarranted after recent revelations of massive cheating by schools to meet NCLB performance goals.) One part of NCLB, the Reading First program, offered extra money to states on the condition that their schools only use programs and curricula approved by the Bush administration's Education Department. Let's not mince words about President Bush's NCLB: this education reform *really* was all about federal "bribes" and coercion of states and localities.

Yet NCLB passed in the U.S. Senate by 87 percent, with only three Republicans voting no; and in the House of Representatives by 88 percent, with only 33 Republicans voting no. Very few of the conservative critics and politicians now attacking the Common Core for the sin of federal dictation of education policies have ever protested the imposition on the states of the far more restrictive NCLB mandates. Most critics haven't even acknowledged that NCLB went miles further along the road to federal control of education than anything called for in the Common Core Standards.

The issue isn't merely that some of the critics and Republican politicians appear to be guilty of hypocrisy. It is that the conservatives' obsession with the "illegality" of Common Core has distorted the education reform conversation, making it more difficult to have the informed debate the country now needs about the educational quality of the Common Core Standards and its actual effect in the classroom – the "primal scene" of education reform.

I accept as a given that the Common Core hasn't yet proved itself. (How could it in two to three years?) That's why the public needs to know more about what the states, our "laboratories of democracy," are actually doing on a daily basis to implement the standards in schools and classrooms. Assessing that information and having that conversation is undermined when conservatives – with virtually no supporting evidence – continue to loudly insist that the Common Core project is nothing but an illegal federal power grab. In the Manichean view of the Tea Party and many movement conservatives, Americans have only one choice to make about the Common Core Standards: either defend our constitutional republic's tradition of local control of the schools or surrender abjectly to the federal government's "Obamacore" takeover.

Even some thoughtful public intellectuals have fallen into that conversation-ending trap. Consider the following comments on a Fox News panel by popular conservative columnist George Will:

> *[Common Core] is a thin end of an enormous wedge of federal power that will be wielded for the constant progressive purpose of concentrating power in Washington so that it can impose continental solutions to problems nationwide. You say it's voluntary. It has been driven by the use of*

*bribes and coercion in the form of waivers from
No Child Left Behind or Race to the Top money
to buy the compliance of these 45 states, two of
which — Indiana and I believe Oklahoma — have
already backed out, and they will not be the last.*

To his credit, Will was one of the few conservatives to criticize the federal overreach in NCLB. But he was apparently unaware that there was far less use of "federal power" by the Obama administration in support of the Common Core than there was by the Bush administration in imposing NCLB on the states. Will also contradicted himself by arguing that the Obama administration forced Common Core on the states through "bribes and coercion," while trumpeting the fact that seven states have resisted the administration. Conservatives can't have it both ways — applauding every state defection from the Common Core but continuing to repeat the fiction that this is an unbreakable federal imposition on the states.

Despite the constant drumbeat about the

"illegal" federal education takeover behind the Common Core, there is virtually no serious scholarship supporting that accusation. The only effort that qualifies as somewhat research-based is a policy brief that criticizes the Common Core published by the conservative Pioneer Institute in Boston. The paper argues that the standards were forced on the states in violation of established constitutional principles and statutory law. According to the two lawyers who authored the paper, "In three short years, the present administration has placed the nation on the road to a national curriculum." However, there's no background history in this "research" paper, no mention of the quarter-century of advocacy for national standards by leading American education reformers, including many conservatives. There's only the sudden, arbitrary education coup pulled off by the Obama administration leading to the imposition of the Common Core Standards on the states.

The pretentiously named "white paper" is nothing more than a bluff. Lawyers make arguments all the time about the meaning of the Constitution and federal laws. That's one of the things they do for their paying clients. But what makes a legal claim true or not true is not what lawyers say but rather what judges and juries decide in a court of law. With so many disgruntled parents and teachers available for a class-action lawsuit, you might think that the Pioneer Institute (or any of the other anti-Common Core groups) would be eager to test the argument of illegality in a court of law. The fact that they haven't done so suggests that they realize they would be laughed out of court.

IV

The tragedy in the conservative assault over "illegal Obamacore" is that it undermines serious public discussion and inquiry about the most pressing question in American education today. The question is this: Can Common Core, with all its faults, still lead to significant improvement in the quality of instruction in the nation's classrooms? You wouldn't know it from the incessant complaints, but the Common Core document includes a breakthrough declaration about revolutionizing classroom instruction that is perfectly consistent with conservative (or traditional) education principles. If implemented properly, that declaration might lead to academic gains for American students. It appears on page 6 of the Common Core State Standards for English Language Arts:

While the Standards make reference to some particular forms of content, including mythology, foundational U.S. documents, and Shakespeare, they do not – indeed cannot – enumerate all or even most of the content that students should learn. The Standards must therefore be complemented by a well-developed, content-rich curriculum consistent with the expectations laid out in this document.

Fordham Institute scholar Robert Pondiscio refers to the content-knowledge passage as the "58 most important words in education reform today." That's because everything hinges on whether the states and school districts actually develop a "content-rich curriculum" for the schools. In turn, that would break the stranglehold the progressive education movement has had on classroom instruction for more than a half-century.

It's impossible to exaggerate the significance of these words appearing in a national standards document that 43 states are now pledged to implement. With the exception of Massachusetts's 1993 Education Reform Act (also heavily influenced by E. D. Hirsch's ideas) no other state's standards have ever explicitly called for a content-knowledge curriculum. Moreover many of the grade-level standards expect students to engage with specific content and broaden their historical and cultural literacy. For example, students in ninth and 10th grades are asked to "analyze seminal U.S. documents of historical and literary significance (e.g., Washington's Farewell Address, the Gettysburg Address, Roosevelt's Four Freedoms speech, King's 'Letter from Birmingham Jail'), including how they address related themes and concepts."

The passage about content knowledge constitutes acknowledgment by the Common Core writers that E. D. Hirsch's historic

---

Conservative and leftist critiques of Common Core now often overlap into one unified conspiracy theory.

---

critique of progressive education, along with his call for restoration of a content-based, grade-by-grade curriculum, has been vindicated by the evidence. Thus it is worth mentioning that Common Core's call for a coherent curriculum was inserted into the standards after lead writer David Coleman held consultations with Professor Hirsch.

It is true that neither Hirsch nor Core Knowledge is mentioned in the key passage, or anywhere else in the standards. The omission was deliberate and entirely strategic. The authors were acutely aware that U.S. education law forbids the federal government from creating curricula for the schools. (Never mind that in the case of NCLB's Reading First program, the Bush administration willfully ignored the prohibition.) Even though Common Core began as a private initiative, Coleman and the other writers knew they were walking a political tightrope regarding the curriculum issue. (Imagine the outcry from conservative activists if the Common Core actually did include a preference for a particular curriculum.)

Thus, despite the Common Core authors' appreciation for Hirsch's approach to classroom instruction, the curriculum message had to be implicit rather than explicit. The decision to omit a reference to any particular curriculum was, in the circumstances, understandable. But it also had the unintended consequence that the directive to choose a "well-developed, content-rich curriculum" came with no teeth – that is, with no enforcement mechanism in the states. In turn, that's one more proof of the absurdity of the critics' claims that the Obama administration is using Common Core to impose a "federalized curriculum" on the states.

As state education boards adopted the Common Core and soon began grappling with the complexities of curriculum selection, the federal Education Department was never a player. Indeed, no recognized education authority offered guidance to the states to make sure that they were truly complying with the Common Core's call for a "well-developed, content-rich curriculum." Individual states had to (and still have to) figure out the curriculum piece on their own.

This inevitably created a muddle, as commercial curriculum providers and publishers – even those that previously claimed to be honoring progressive education approaches to instruction – now came forward to claim that their products were "Common Core aligned" in order to boost their chances of winning contracts from the states. Without any objective authority to guide the states, who was to say that the publishers were wrong in their claims of Common Core alignment?

Critics point to these vagaries in the curriculum selection process to question the educational value of the Common Core. But the fact that such uncertainty exists also disproves the critics' claim that the Obama administration set up the Common Core in order to impose a national curriculum on the schools. For the sake of beleaguered state and local officials who are now grappling with the curriculum issue, one almost wishes that U.S. Secretary of Education Arne Duncan actually had the power to step in and force states to settle on one or two curriculum choices that qualify under Common Core's criterion of "rich content knowledge." That's actually the way it's done in most other nations that consistently outperform the U.S. in educational achievement.

V

As they celebrate their victories in several states, conservative Common Core opponents will have to take responsibility for what they have wrought and declare what they are now in favor of. Unfortunately, the critics seem too busy to notice what's actually happening in classrooms. The critics – at least most of them – still prefer to fly above the real battleground, where schools and teachers will now determine whether Common Core's instructional guidelines will lead to improved academic outcomes. Instead of entering that contested arena and lending their weight to the struggle for the proper teaching of reading, more academic content knowledge and a curriculum favorable to American republican values, most conservative education critics seem content to lob their ideological grenades against "Obamacore," which still exists in 43 states.

You can see this conservative abdication more clearly by looking at what happened in

New York State and New York City in the years before and after the advent of the Common Core Standards. The state was first in the nation to sign on to the standards and did so with great enthusiasm. The city has the biggest school district in the country, with 1,800 schools and a million-plus students. Until the Common Core, Gotham was a solid bastion of progressive education.

The city became a laboratory for examining the deformities of progressive education when its schools came under mayoral control – that is, totally centralized control – after

---

Despite the constant drumbeat about the "illegal" federal education takeover behind the Common Core, there is virtually no serious scholarship supporting that accusation.

---

the election of Michael Bloomberg in 2001. With little background in instructional issues, Mayor Bloomberg and his new Schools Chancellor Joel Klein deferred most decisionmaking in the area of classroom instruction to a cadre of veteran progressive educators, who in turn championed the progressive "balanced literacy" reading and writing program developed by Professor Lucy Calkins of Columbia Teachers College.

Deputy Chancellor Carmen Fariña, a good friend and collaborator of Calkins's, became the education department's enforcer, making sure that virtually all teachers in the elementary schools toed the line in carrying out Calkins's constructivist methods for teaching reading and writing.

Balanced literacy has no track record of raising the academic performance of poor minority children. No independent research study has ever evaluated its methodology. Nevertheless, it was popular in education schools because it promulgated two of progressive education's key commandments: that teachers must abandon deadening "drill and kill" methods and that students are capable of "constructing their own knowledge." Progressives such as Calkins evoke ideal classrooms, where young children naturally find their way to literacy without enduring boring, scripted phonics drills. Instead, in a balanced-literacy classroom, students work in small groups and follow what Calkins calls the "workshop model" of cooperative learning.

Fariña and Calkins managed to create the most centralized, top-down instructional system in the recent history of American public education. Fariña's agents (euphemistically called coaches) fanned out to almost all elementary schools to make sure that every teacher was marching in lockstep with the progressive approach. Calkins's balanced literacy was enforced with draconian discipline in city schools for several years.

Progressives like Calkins and Fariña don't insist that more learning occurs when children work in groups and in "natural" settings because they've followed the evidence. To the contrary, science makes clear that – particularly for disadvantaged children – direct, explicit instruction works best.

Nevertheless, under Fariña, re-education sessions for teachers were meant to overcome dissenting opinion and drive home the progressive party line. To quote the directives to teachers included in one education department manual: "Your students must not be sitting in rows. You must not stand at the head of the class. You must not do 'chalk and talk' at the blackboard. You must have a 'workshop' in every single reading period. Your students must be 'active learners,' and they must work in groups."

But balanced literacy was an abject failure. The city's eighth-grade reading scores on the NAEP tests barely budged over 12 years, despite a doubling of education spending – from $12 billion to $24 billion. There was no narrowing of the racial achievement gap.

Recognizing balanced literacy's meager results, Chancellor Klein set up a three-year pilot program, matching 10 elementary schools using the Hirsch early-grade literacy curriculum against a demographically similar cohort of 10 schools that used balanced literacy. The children in the Core Knowledge schools significantly outperformed those in the schools using the Calkins approach. By the time he left the department in 2009, Klein had become a supporter of Hirsch's Core Knowledge curriculum, with its focus on direct instruction and the teaching of broad content knowledge.

The following year, New York State committed to implementing the new Common Core Standards. Since Calkins's balanced literacy was not properly aligned to the new standards, particularly Common Core's emphasis on content knowledge, the progressive education program was soon pushed to the margins. The state education department selected Hirsch's Core Knowledge Foundation to write a "content-rich curriculum" as specified in the standards for pre-K through second grade. The curriculum was then posted on the state education department's website and made available for use by all schools in the state — though there was no requirement for any school to choose the state-recommended curriculum.

The city's education department followed suit. It made Core Knowledge one of its recommended curricula for the early grades. Balanced literacy was now left off the recommended list. Nevertheless, neither the state nor the city forced the schools to follow its curriculum recommendations. Still, 71 city elementary schools chose the Core Knowledge curriculum. It was the biggest leap ever for the Hirsch curriculum and a portent of what might happen elsewhere if Common Core's declaration in favor of a content-knowledge curriculum were taken seriously by other states.

But wait, nothing is ever settled in American education. Last year, Gotham's voters elected Bill de Blasio, a political progressive, as their new mayor. He in turn brought back the *education* progressive Carmen Fariña as his new schools chancellor. It took all of six months on the job for Fariña to declare that Common Core Standards or not, the pilot study proving the superior performance of Core Knowledge or not, Lucy Calkins's balanced literacy was coming back to city classrooms.

New York City is thus likely to become a major battlefield in a new round of the reading wars, as well as a test of the meaning of the Common Core. Can progressive education reclaim its hegemony in the city, or will the schools (at least some of them) choose an academically serious curriculum for the children? The feds, of course, will have no influence on the outcome of that struggle.

In New York City, at least, conservative education activists now face a consequential choice: Will they continue fighting the last ideological war over the alleged federal imposition of Common Core? Or will they now see the Common Core, with its admitted limitations, as a framework and a wedge to counteract progressives like Fariña and Calkins, who again want to foist a dumbed-

The Common Core document includes a breakthrough declaration about revolutionizing classroom instruction that is perfectly consistent with conservative (or traditional) education principles.

down, unproven education program on the city's 1 million children? One would hope that regardless of their original – and now disproven – theories about Common Core and illegal federal control, conservative reformers will support proper classroom instruction and an academic curriculum that is each American child's birthright.

First American edition published in 2014 by Encounter Books, an activity of Encounter for Culture and Education, Inc., a nonprofit, tax exempt corporation.
Encounter Books website address: www.encounterbooks.com

Manufactured in the United States and printed on acid-free paper. The paper used in this publication meets the minimum requirements of ANSI/NISO Z39.48–1992 (R 1997) (*Permanence of Paper*).

FIRST AMERICAN EDITION

LIBRARY OF CONGRESS CATALOGING-IN-PUBLICATION DATA

Stern, Sol, 1935–
Common core : yea & nay / by Sol Stern & Peter W. Wood.
pages   cm. — (Encounter broadsides ; 40)
Includes bibliographical references.
ISBN 978-1-59403-819-8 (PAPERBACK) —
ISBN 978-1-59403-820-4 (ebook)
1. Education—Standards—United States. 2. Education—Curricula—Standards—United States. 3. Academic achievement—United States. 4. Educational evaluation—United States. I. Wood, Peter, 1953–
II. Title.
LB3060.83.S84 2014
379.1580973—dc23
2014031707

10 9 8 7 6 5 4 3 2 1

Why the Common Core
Is a Bad Idea

The political fortunes of the Common Core are fast changing. When the Common Core first caught public attention in early 2010, it seemed like an unstoppable locomotive. It had the support of President Obama, and within a matter of a few months, 40 states and the District of Columbia had formally adopted it. Six more states would soon follow. Republican and Democratic governors endorsed it. The Common Core was roaring ahead not just with bipartisan political support but also with widespread enthusiasm from teachers unions, the press, and much of the D.C.-based education establishment.

As I write in the summer of 2014, the prospect is a bit different. That locomotive is nowhere to be seen and may be lying on its side in a dry gulch.

Consider: The American Federation of Teachers (AFT), the country's second largest

teachers union, is in full retreat from its earlier commitment to the Common Core. A June 2014 Rasmussen national poll of 1,000 adults showed that only a third of adults who have children support the Common Core – an 18-point drop since November 2013.

Indiana, South Carolina, Louisiana, and Oklahoma have withdrawn from the Common Core. Missouri, Ohio, and Wisconsin are debating whether to withdraw. North Carolina turned aside an effort to repeal the standards but appointed a commission to undertake a "comprehensive" review of them. Utah's governor has asked the state attorney general to look at "federal entanglements" that may have been part of the state's adoption of the Common Core. The governor of

The proponents of the Common Core are in retreat and fighting a defensive battle.

Mississippi has switched from a Common Core advocate to an opponent. Eleven states (Utah, Alabama, Pennsylvania, Oklahoma, Georgia, Indiana, Florida, Kansas, Kentucky, Alaska, and Tennessee) have exited from the testing consortia that are integral to Common Core. Michigan and North Carolina are deciding whether to follow suit.

The National Governors Association, which co-founded the Common Core in 2008, just held its annual meeting in Nashville and didn't even put the Common Core on its official agenda because, as one of the governors put it, the topic has become too "divisive." Iowa Governor Terry Branstad, a Common Core backer, told the Associated Press that the words *Common Core* are "radioactive."

Jeb Bush, who pinned his 2016 presidential hopes to his strong support for the Common Core, finds himself isolated from a large swath of Republican voters. Town-hall meetings across the country are crowded with parents and teachers who are making common cause against the Common Core. What some have

dubbed a "populist revolt" is under way. And at least one of the principal supporters of the Common Core is taking heed: Bill Gates is having second thoughts. In June, the Bill & Melinda Gates Foundation called for a two-year moratorium on any states or school districts basing high-stakes decisions on the results of the Common Core-aligned standardized tests. Without the tests, the Common Core is educational vapor – the steam emanating from that wrecked locomotive lying in the ditch.

Doubts about the Common Core are registering most vividly, but not exclusively, in Republican politics. Some erstwhile Republican supporters of the Common Core, such as Louisiana Governor Bobby Jindal and Oklahoma Governor Mary Fallin, have switched sides. Other Republican leaders, such as Senators Rand Paul, Ted Cruz, and Marco Rubio, are outspoken opponents, as are Mike Huckabee, Rick Santorum, Texas Governor Rick Perry, Indiana Governor Mike Pence, and South Carolina Governor Nikki Haley. Other

Republicans, like Wisconsin Governor Scott Walker, are straddling the issue. New Jersey Governor Chris Christie recently said he's going to issue an executive order to attempt to address parents' numerous concerns about Common Core.

Meanwhile, prominent Democratic leaders are attempting to find a workable position, caught between President Obama's support for the Common Core and the disaffection of many teachers who are part of the party's progressive base. No nationally important Democrats have spoken out against the Common Core, but many have trimmed their sails in light of the pushback from the teachers unions. Not only has the AFT bailed, but the nation's largest teachers union, the National Education Association (NEA), has also called for the resignation of U.S. Secretary of Education Arne Duncan. The NEA has gripes with the Obama administration beyond the Common Core, but the high-stakes testing that is part of the Common Core is at the top of their list.

To call this a train wreck, of course, may be an exaggeration. The Common Core still has supporters, not least President Obama. And the backtracking I've described has many zigs and zags. The president of the AFT, Randi Weingarten, gave an opening address to the union's convention in which she sought middle ground. Some union members, she said, believe "the [Common Core] standards should be jettisoned," and "some of you, myself included, think they hold great promise, but they've been implemented terribly." In that light, she offered her support for teachers who want to improve or modify the standards. This would leave the AFT officially in favor of Common Core but would allow dissenting teachers to oppose it as publicly as they would like. The AFT was also poised to consider some resolutions that would go far beyond Weingarten's compromise by declaring outright rejection of the Common Core.

While the list of Republicans who oppose the Common Core is long and growing, there

are still prominent figures such as Jeb Bush who support it unwaveringly. Among these is Louisiana Senator Thad Cochran, who narrowly defeated Common Core opponent and Tea Party activist Chris McDaniel in a (still disputed) primary race.

By the time these words reach print, these ripped-from-the-headlines stories will be replaced by new ones, but they will follow suit. The proponents of the Common Core are in retreat and fighting a defensive battle. Their dream of a one-size-fits-all set of national educational standards integrated with meaningful national tests is in ruins. The best they can now hope for is a remnant of the original idea: a handful of stalwart blue states that stick with the Core and a delayed and then watered-down system of tests.

Good Idea, Bad Implementation?

To say that the larger project has failed the test of political support and public popularity, however, doesn't necessarily mean that the

Common Core was a bad idea. Could Randi Weingarten be right when she says the Common Core was a great idea marred by poor implementation? In a word, no.

The Common Core was never a good idea. It was a sneaky idea – and sneaky ideas in American public policy tend to have exactly the life span that Common Core has had. They emerge seemingly from out of nowhere and initially appear wholesome and without blemish. They rise meteorically without any real opposition. Then a few suspicious souls start to ask questions. And as the details materialize, the suspicions spread and begin to harden into opposition. And the opposition feeds on the sense of many people that someone has tried to dupe them. Because someone has.

To speak of the Common Core as sneaky and involving an attempt to dupe people, of course, implies that the proponents were not acting in good faith. Indeed, I think *some* of the Common Core proponents could be fairly described as so determined to advance

what they believed to be a good idea that they knowingly cut corners, evaded proper public scrutiny for their proposal, and attempted to cement it into place before anyone quite understood what it would entail. Their maneuvers might be described as admirably shrewd in that age-old "Never mind the fine print, sign here" manner.

The Common Core hustlers, however, were a small part of the Common Core coalition. Most of the Common Core supporters acted in perfectly good faith. They simply bought what the hustlers sold them and went out to tell their friends and neighbors that a wonderful thing was coming their way. These supporters can be accused of credulity, or even stubborn credulity, but they were not sneaky.

Sneakiness first, then credulity.

CORE SNEAKINESS

The core sneakiness of the Common Core is that it was (and still is) presented as a state-level project when it was from the get-go

intended to be a national project. Its official name is the Common Core K-12 *State* Standards, but the reality is that Common Core is designed to work as a de facto set of *national* standards.

This isn't the only sneakiness. The attempt to frame the Common Core as a state-level project was motivated by the need to evade federal law and constitutional barriers to federal efforts to regulate public schools' standards, curricula, and testing.

The proponents of the Common Core insist, often vehemently, that it is simply a set of "standards" and not a "curriculum." It is, in fact, very much a curriculum. The sneakiness in this case is again aimed at getting around legal barriers that prohibit federal efforts to establish curricula, but the sneakiness is also aimed at diverting teachers and the public from the truth. The word *standards* suggests high-level guidelines that allow schools and teachers to fill in the details. The word *curriculum* suggests much more nuts-and-bolts specifications at the school level. There is no

sharp line that divides standards and curricula. The more specific standards become, the more they merge into a curriculum. The Common Core standards are finely detailed, grade-by-grade specifications for what should be taught, how it should be taught, and when it should be taught.

The Common Core State Standards Initiative maintains a Myths vs. Facts web page

---

The Common Core was never a good idea. It was a sneaky idea.

---

that includes the assertion, "The Common Core is *not* a curriculum," and elaborates, "Teachers will continue to devise lesson plans and tailor instruction to the individual needs of the students in their classrooms." This assertion is echoed in promotional material about the Common Core across the country. Even the U.S. Department of Education goes out of its way to say that the Common Core

is "standards," not a "curriculum." No amount of repetition, however, will make this statement true. If it walks and talks like a curriculum, it *is* a curriculum, even if it has some fill-in-the-blank components that allow teachers limited discretion.

Perhaps the strongest proof that the "standards" are a curriculum in disguise comes at the next layer of sneakiness, the Common Core-aligned tests. For no matter how creative teachers are in supplementing what the Common Core Standards mandate, in the end, they have to prepare their students for the tests, and the testmakers have no interest in anything teachers add to the Core.

The Common Core was designed from the outset to be integrated with a set of tests. To that end, two separate testing consortia were created: the Smarter Balanced Assessment Consortium (SBAC) and the Partnership for Assessment of Readiness for College and Careers (PARCC). The most important thing to know about SBAC and PARCC is that they are private organizations outside

the control of local and state authorities but with the potential to wield enormous influence over the schools. SBAC and PARCC, as originally conceived, determine the questions that will be asked on Common Core exams. The content of the exams, of course, inevitably drives what the teachers teach. That's because the teachers want their students to succeed, but it is also because the teachers themselves will be rewarded or punished on the basis of how well their students perform on the tests. Teacher apprehension about how the test results will be used in teacher evaluation is reflected in the demand made by NEA president Dennis Van Roekel in February 2014 for a two-year moratorium on using the tests in that way.

So when the Common Core proponents say that the "standards" are just high-level ideals and the schools and teachers can decide for themselves the actual content of the curricula, those proponents are being sneaky. They know full well that the teachers will have to "teach to the tests" and that the tests

will reinforce the Common Core's top-down vision of American education. The growing opposition from teachers and teachers unions centers on this point. Moreover, the test creators, SBAC and PARCC, have also been encouraged by the Department of Education to develop curricular and instructional materials for Common Core in addition to the tests.

The sneakiness doesn't stop there. The Common Core, as implemented by the U.S. Department of Education, is intertwined with another Obama initiative called the Statewide Longitudinal Data System (SLDS). SLDS, like the Common Core, was part of the Race to the Top, and both were part of the 2009 State Fiscal Stabilization Fund (A.K.A. the "stimulus"). Race to the Top was a U.S. Education Department program that created a competition among states for a share of a $4.35 billion package. To compete, states had to commit to adopting specific K-12 reforms in math and English that just so happened to be identical to the Common Core.

The basic idea of SLDS was to collect a

massive amount of data on all students in American public schools and track each student year by year from kindergarten through high school. The idea was enthusiastically taken up by the testing consortium PARCC and its parent body Achieve Inc., except that Achieve wasn't content with only K-12 tracking. It proposed to extend the data collection from preschool through graduate school. Other companies presented themselves as ready to help, including the data-mining expert inBloom. To be clear, the plan for data mining wasn't part of the Common Core itself, but they quickly became fused, and both were seen by the Department of Education as parts of a single initiative.

When the public caught wind of this new component of the Common Core, there was a hue and cry, and the Common Core advocates beat a hasty retreat. Several states, such as Oklahoma and Georgia, passed legislation or issued executive orders aimed at protecting students from the system. Whether it has really gone away remains to be seen. The idea that

"state" standards would lead to a system of private organizations in possession of material for data mining the entire schooling of individual children is appalling – and yet entirely consistent with the national-surveillance mentality of the Common Core. The extent of the data mining is controversial, but it is clear that it is part of the overall plan for institutionalizing the Core.

The federal involvement with data mining takes us back to the original point: the Common Core is profoundly a federal initiative. It is a federal initiative dressed up as a collection of initiatives by the states, but the motley collection of straw hats, snowshoes, coveralls, and bikinis are just props. The real actors are the suits in Washington.

MOVING THE COUCH

If the Common Core were such a good idea, why did its original proponents resort to subterfuge? The short answer: frustration. For

decades, would-be reformers of American schools had sought to use the powers of the federal government to overcome the deficiencies in our schools. Those deficiencies are as old or older than the republic itself. Americans have always struggled to find better ways to educate our children. In the 1830s, Horace Mann thought that professionally educated teachers would improve the situation. John Dewey helped launch the progressive-education movement in the 1880s, with its emphasis on cultivating the child's own interests. The 1983 report, *A Nation at Risk: The Imperative for Educational Reform,* is the conventional starting point for the contemporary school-reform movement. It enunciated the idea that the quality of American schools had fallen far below the level of schools in other developed nations. And it set in motion numerous efforts to "raise standards" and "improve performance."

These seem to be intractable problems for the United States. Here and there we make

some progress, but the general picture seldom improves much or for long. There are many reasons for this, and it is a list with something to offend everyone. We have:

- Schools of education that emphasize pedagogy over substance and generally do a poor job of preparing teachers

- Teachers unions that protect incompetent teachers

- Regional differences in the United States, in which some regions put much more emphasis on intellectual accomplishment than others

- A racial achievement gap linked to communities that put a low value on academic achievement or stigmatize it as "acting white"

- Poor, crime-ridden neighborhoods with low social capital

- Large numbers of unassimilated or poorly assimilated immigrants

> The rapid increase in single-parent households, which correlates closely with poor academic performance by the children

> High geographic mobility, which disrupts students' education

> A national ethos that values education as practical training more than it values intellectual striving

> A strong tradition of local control over schools

The would-be reformer who sets out to improve American schools confronts a nation that often says it wants better education but is unable or unwilling to do much about any of these things. Ronald Reagan campaigned in 1980 on the idea that he would close President Jimmy Carter's "gift to the teachers unions," the newly formed Department of Education. Reagan failed. Schools of education have been the academic cellar of university programs for more than half a century,

but they are also profit centers, partly because they offer rungs up the ladder of professional

---

The core sneakiness of the Common Core is that it was (and still is) presented as a state-level project.

---

advancement for teachers. Politicians relentlessly assail the racial achievement gap with new programs but typically come to rest on "institutional racism" explanations and pay no attention to the culture of underachievement. And so it goes.

When confronted with problems we can't or won't fix, we are tempted to focus on the problems we can fix. If we can't move the walls, we can move the couch and rearrange the chairs. That's how Common Core got started. What the reformers really wanted was a national curriculum embodying high

standards and backed with the muscle of the federal government. If only they had that, they reasoned, they could fix at least some of those seemingly intractable problems. With a single national standard, for example, we could ensure that schools of education in every state could prepare would-be teachers for a uniformly high level. The geographic mobility of students would cease to be an issue because the standards and the content would be the same everywhere. The national curriculum might even help overcome the racial achievement gap by ensuring that students in inner-city schools get taught to the same standard as students in affluent suburban schools.

That, in any case, was the dream. But making it happen was never going to be easy. It meant overcoming the tradition of state and local control of schools – a tradition rooted in the Constitution that left education to the states, and a tradition later enshrined in statutory law, beginning with the 1965 Elementary and Secondary Education Act. The latter

specified that "nothing in this act" shall authorize any federal official to "mandate, direct, or control" the curriculum of a state, local educational agency, or school. The substance of this restriction was repeated in the General Education Provisions Act of 1970, the Department of Education Organization Act of 1979, and the No Child Left Behind Act of 2001. None of these laws was ever repealed or superseded. By law, the United States government is prohibited from doing the things that the reformers most wanted: to establish national standards, testing, and a curriculum.

President George W. Bush's No Child Left Behind (NCLB) law probably went as far in the direction of federal involvement as the law would allow. NCLB insisted that states establish rigorous standards, and it threatened schools that failed to live up to those standards. But it left the states free to choose their own standards and their own tests. NCLB had some noticeably beneficial effects, but it

also became notorious for its flaws. Teachers complained strenuously that the regimen of tests forced them to drill students on testable items rather than pursue more meaningful education. And numerous schools were caught in cheating scandals. Rather than risk being punished for failing to meet NCLB benchmarks of progress, some schools handed out answers or doctored the results.

Toward the end of the Bush presidency, the reformers had lost whatever hope they had that NCLB would be their ticket to a national curriculum. And this is where David Coleman, the architect of the Common Core, had his moment of genius. He thought of a possible way around the restrictions on creating a national curriculum. It had two elements: wordplay and evasive maneuver. The wordplay consisted of calling the curriculum "standards." The evasion was to engineer the adoption of the "standards" on a state-by-state basis.

* * *

The detailed history of how the Common Core came about deserves to be told, and it deserves to be told by someone other than an acolyte. But here I have space for only a short sketch. David Coleman, the son of a former president of Bennington College, graduated from Yale and went as a Rhodes Scholar to both Oxford and Cambridge. In 2000 he co-founded the Grow Network, which aimed to make "assessment" (i.e., testing) more useful to teachers, parents, and students. The Grow Network was bought by McGraw-Hill in 2004. His critics have often pointed to the irony that the most influential modern reformer of public schools has very little actual experience with them. As an undergraduate, he tutored in a New Haven, Conn., public school. Other than that, he spent his early career as a consultant and now serves as president of the College Board.

In 2007 Coleman co-founded Student Achievement Partners (SAP), the nonprofit

that took the lead in designing the English Language Arts and Mathematics sections of the Common Core. SAP was funded by contracts with the Bill & Melinda Gates Foundation. Coleman received help in founding SAP from Susan Pimentel, who is widely identified as another lead author of the Common Core. She spent most of her career as an education analyst, working as an independent consultant for state and district boards of education. She works with initiatives such as Achieve's American Diploma Project, which aims to make high school curricula preparatory for job and college expectations; and the National Assessment Governing Board, which oversees Congress's National Assessment of Educational Progress (A.K.A. the Nation's Report Card). She also co-founded the nonprofit educational consultancy StandardsWork to help policymakers and school districts understand and use standards and testing.

The third figure at the root of the Common Core tree is Jason Zimba, currently a physics and mathematics professor at Bennington

College (where Coleman's mother served as president from 1987 to 2013). Zimba and two others wrote the mathematics portion of the Common Core standards. He too was a Rhodes Scholar at Oxford, where he earned a master's degree in mathematics in 1993, and he earned a PhD in physics from the University of California, Berkeley, in 2001. In 2007 he and Coleman co-wrote a paper for the Carnegie Corporation on mathematics standards, and he also was a co-founder – along with Coleman – of the Grow Network. Zimba's responsibilities focused on standards alignment, curriculum design, product development, educational strategy, and psychometrics. Along with Coleman and Pimentel, he is also the third founder of Student Achievement Partners.

Coleman, Pimentel, and Zimba are the inner core of the Common Core. Without them, there would be no Common Core. The three are clearly closely connected with one another and the same handful of organizations, and Student Achievement Partners

> *When confronted with problems we can't or won't fix, we are tempted to focus on the problems we can fix.*

was the mother of the Common Core. Several of the other key players in the promotion and implementation of the Common Core are also partners in SAP.

Inventing the idea of the Common Core, of course, meant nothing without a mechanism to promote it. The key to that was Gene Wilhoit, who spearheaded the development and adoption of the Common Core while serving as executive director of the Council of Chief State School Officers, the organization that, along with the National Governors Association, created and now owns the Common Core State Standards. Wilhoit left the council in summer 2012 to become executive director of the University of Kentucky's

National Center for Innovation in Education, a new Gates-funded organization developed to help states comply with the Common Core and to ensure that all 50 states adopt uniform definitions of "college- and career-readiness."

After Coleman left his position as CEO of SAP to head the College Board, Wilhoit joined as a partner with Pimentel and Zimba. Wilhoit also joined the board of inBloom, a Gates Foundation-funded nonprofit database company, which will handle data collection and tracking of sensitive information for schoolchildren as part of the Common Core's reshaping of K-12 education. Wilhoit has a long career in education management and state bureaucracy, including serving as the education commissioner in Kentucky and in Arkansas (where he championed assessments and accountability systems), as a program director in the Indiana Department of Education, as a school administrator in Kanawha County, W.V., as a special assistant in the U.S. Department of Education, and as the execu-

tive director of the National Association of State Boards of Education. He holds degrees from Georgetown College and Indiana University and has also studied education administration at the West Virginia College of Graduate Studies. He is also one of the few creators of the Common Core with any teaching experience, having started his career as a social-sciences teacher in Ohio and Indiana.

Coleman has extolled Wilhoit as "an educational hero" who "understood the need for this country to better prepare *all* students for life beyond high school and he had the distinctive intelligence, persistence and political skill to bring an amazing set of academic standards to life."

The circle of people involved in the creation and promotion of the Common Core widens rapidly from these four, and in the interest of brevity, I'll turn to the institutional side. In 2008, two private organizations, the Council of Chief State School Officers and the National Governors Association

(NGA), urged the development of national education standards. Achieve, a private education nonprofit, joined in the movement, and the James B. Hunt Institute helped by sponsoring conferences and summits for state education leaders and officials. Hunt was the Democratic governor of North Carolina (1977–85, 1993–2001) and hosted an NGA conference on the Common Core in June 2008 to boost other current and former governors' interest in the project.

Six months later, the Council of Chief State School Officers, NGA, and Achieve issued a formal call for the development of national K-12 standards, which set in motion the writing of the Common Core.

In July 2009, President Obama and U.S. Secretary of Education Arne Duncan announced Race to the Top, the federally sponsored state education competition incentivizing the adoption of Common Core. This was four months before states had their first peek at the first draft of the standards and 11 months before the standards were finished. Forty-one

states applied for Race to the Top money in Phase 1 of applications, due January 2010. At that time, an early draft of the standards had been released to the public just two months prior, and the validation committee had met only once. (They would meet twice more to review new iterations of the standards.)

Phase 2 applications were due on June 1, 2010, the day final Common Core State Standards were released to the states and one day before the standards were released to the public. In November and December 2011, states had the opportunity to complete a two-part application for Phase 3 of Race to the Top funding, just five months after the final standards were made public.

The Common Core might well have attracted and held the attention of a handful of states without the Race to the Top, but it would clearly not have gained anything like the formal support of 46 states, nearly all of which adopted it sight unseen as the price of a sweepstakes ticket for the Race to the Top funds.

As an exercise in lawmaking, the adoption of the Common Core by those 46 states stands as one of the worst examples of malfeasance in modern American history. Within a matter of a few months, most Americans were placed under a new nationalized educational regime they had no share in creating and no opportunity to review. There were no bills, hearings, or debates in Congress or in state legislatures. Many states acted blindly in the hope that the Race to the Top funds would be worth it at a time of straitened state budgets. In most states, the matter was handled directly by commissioners and boards of education. Democracy and representative government blinked. David Coleman won.

A Conspiracy of Duncans

Of course it didn't end there. A few states, notably Texas, resisted the initial temptation to sign up. Others soon began to look at the pig in a poke and didn't like what they saw. As for the "state" standards being voluntary,

legislators and governors in states that had buyer's remorse soon found themselves threatened by Secretary of Education Duncan, who held to the view that they had no right to back out of the Common Core once their states had opted in. In February 2012, Duncan called criticisms of the Common Core State Standards "a conspiracy theory in search of a conspiracy." When South Carolina legislators awoke to the reality that their state was expected to pay 90 percent of the costs of the Common Core and began to look for the exits, Duncan derided them:

I hope South Carolina lawmakers will heed the voices of teachers who supported South Carolina's decision to stop lowering academic standards and set a higher bar for success. And I hope lawmakers will continue to support the state's decision to raise standards, with the goal of making every child college- and career-ready in today's knowledge economy.

His derision of the state's academic standards seemed ill matched to North Carolina's pre-

Common Core rank (by the Fordham Institute, which supports the Common Core) as the state with the best history standards in the nation.

Duncan has proceeded down this path by threatening other states that have wavered in their loyalty to the Common Core. One weapon at Duncan's disposal involves waivers from No Child Left Behind requirements. NCLB conveniently left states vulnerable to a bizarre stipulation that by 2014, "100 percent" of their students would be proficient in math and reading. This, of course, is an impossibility, but schools that fail to achieve that impossibility lose their control of federal funding for disadvantaged children. That's a major budget item for most schools. The Obama administration realized in 2011 that it could weaponize the NCLB rule by promising waivers (unauthorized by Congress) for states it favored and withholding them from other states. The administration went further by breaking the waivers into multiple parts and granting partial and temporary waivers.

So in March 2014, when Indiana became the first state to sign into law a bill taking the state out of the Common Core, the Department of Education's assistant secretary of education, Deb Delisle, promptly sent a letter to Indiana's state superintendent pointing out that Indiana's NCLB waiver was now at risk on the grounds that Indiana's substitute for the Common Core might not be good enough. Delisle reminded Indiana, "The agreement included a promise to have high standards for all students, and federal authorities want proof that the standards the state recently adopted are as challenging as the ones they replaced, known as the Common Core."

David Coleman, meanwhile, has moved from his role as architect of the Common Core to demolition expert for the removal of remaining obstacles. As president of the College Board, he has pledged to align the SATs and the Advanced Placement courses and exams with the Common Core. In spring 2014, he accomplished the SAT realignment by

drastically narrowing the content of the math section, refiguring the verbal section to focus on "evidence-based reading and writing," swapping out vocabulary tests for "relevant words in context," and other adjustments aimed at "propelling students forward."

Some similar ideas lie behind the new radically redesigned Advanced Placement U.S. History standards and exam. The new APUSH, as it is called, has been in the works for a long time and partially predates Coleman's tenure, but like the new SATs, it is imbued with the idea of advancing a certain social program.

The Common Core is not just one thing. It is an educational vision that, followed to its conclusions, calls for changes in every detail of American education, including all of higher education.

Credulity

Earlier in this Broadside I distinguished sneak-iness from credulity, and I have stayed with

the sneakiness so far. Time for the credulity, which means time for Bill Gates. I don't take Gates to be in any way a sneaky man. He is candid about what he wants and sincere in the ways he pursues it. What he wants is a kind of American technocracy in which well-trained utilitarian-minded experts make the key decisions. He has limitless faith in the cult of expertise. He believes the way to get there is to establish limpid standards and enforce them with bureaucratic efficiency.

I take this to be a profoundly misguided view of human nature and an odd misreading of American character, but it is all quite straightforward.

There would be no Common Core without Gates's patronage. He supported David Coleman's startup Student Achievement Partners in 2007, when Coleman was conceptualizing the Common Core. Gates also funded the Council of Chief State School Officers, the organizational platform for Gene Wilhoit, who linked the council with SAP and the National Governors Association.

None of this is sinister. Coleman and Wilhoit simply sized up Gates and spoke to the creator of MS-DOS in terms he could appreciate. The problem with American K-12 education, they told him, was its fragmentary nature. Each state, each school, and even each classroom within each school had its own

The adoption of the Common Core by 46 states stands as one of the worst examples of malfeasance in modern American history.

way of doing things. National standardization is the answer to this chaos. Without standardization, there is no telling what any high school diploma means. And it only makes sense to standardize. Algebra is the same whether you are in Buena Vista, Colo., or Bangor, Maine. Why not teach it in the same way and hold students to the same standards?

Moreover, the lack of standardization hindered the publication of really good textbooks, since the publishers had to address myriad niche markets.

Coleman and Wilhoit had their crucial meeting with Gates in summer 2008. Gates took them seriously, asked some tough questions, and a few weeks later told Wilhoit to count him in. Since then the Bill & Melinda Gates foundation has spent upwards of $200 million to promote the Common Core. As *Washington Post* reporter Lyndsey Layton, whose account of this history I have followed, puts it, "The Gates Foundation spread money across the political spectrum." The beneficiaries included teachers unions, the U.S. Chamber of Commerce, the Center for American Progress, and the Thomas B. Fordham Institute.

Gates's largesse doesn't bear on whether the Common Core is a good idea or a bad idea. It only means that it is a privileged idea – an idea that received less critical attention than it otherwise would have and that

encountered more favorable treatment from typically sluggish institutions.

What money could buy in a policy battle, Gates's money bought. But he probably invested too much in what Coleman and Wilhoit told him in 2008. The Common Core was never destined to bring to America a Gatesian Arcadia of high-performing fellow citizens in love with expertise. And that isn't what Coleman really wanted. The Common Core is essentially a means of educational leveling in the service of centralized state planning and a progressive view of social justice.

A Really Level Playing Field

In the myriad things said about the Common Core and the myriad people saying them, it can be difficult to find the original thread of what the Common Core is all about. But in 2007 — well before Bill Gates went all in, before the Council of Chief State School Officers and the National Governors Association took

it up, before Governor Hunt started to lobby his fellow governors, before Achieve organized as a Common Core content generator, before the Obama administration decided to throw a Common Core log on the stimulus fire and SBAC and PARCC started producing tests, and before inBloom spied the opportunity to mine Common Core data – way back in 2007, David Coleman and his colleague Jason Zimba laid out the real motives of the Common Core. They published a 20-page white paper for the Carnegie Corporation of New York and the Institute for Advanced Study in Princeton, N.J. It was titled "Math and Science Standards That Are Fewer, Clearer, Higher to Raise Achievement at All Levels" and offers a Rosetta stone for the Common Core. Zimba, of course, went on to become the primary author of the Common Core's Mathematics Standards.

In their 2007 paper, Coleman and Zimba laid out, more explicitly than subsequent Common Core documents do, the deep rationale

for what became the Common Core's approach to mathematics. To summarize, their points were:

> The teaching of mathematics in K-12 should be matched to "pragmatic analysis" of what people actually need when they enter the workforce. We shouldn't waste time and effort teaching math that people won't use later.

> Mathematics standards should be chosen to "dramatically" raise "the number and diversity of students performing at the highest levels." To accomplish this would require lowering the definition of "the highest levels." The rhetorical trickery is immediately recognizable. If we define mountains to be elevations of 100 feet above sea level, lots more people can proudly declare themselves to be living on mountaintops. What drove this chicanery was the search for a shortcut to solving the achievement gap between various ethnic groups.

➤ They pressed the motto "Standards that are fewer, clearer, and higher." The motto itself requires so much unpacking that it hardly passes its own test. *Fewer* refers to both the profusion of standards in different states and to the density of standards within states. *Clearer* refers to the claim that existing standards (in 2007) were confusing to both teachers and students. *Higher* is the really mischievous word in the trinity, since it doesn't mean more rigorous, more advanced, more complex, more comprehensive, or more substantively anything. Rather, it seems to mean *easier*. The "higher" standards called for in this report are the standards that will enable a higher percentage of students, especially minority students, to meet them.

In other words, the Common Core takes its origins in what President George W. Bush once called "the soft bigotry of low expectations." Let's not set a single high standard that many students will fail to achieve. Let's

set a single low standard that many will achieve and that we can sell to the public as a "higher standard" in a brand-new sense.

This twisting of the word *higher* to mean its opposite deserves a little further comment. It was an audacious idea. As Coleman and Zimba put it, they advocate for teaching that will result in "true mastery of the essential parts of math and scientific thinking" as opposed to teaching that results in "a weak recall of a vaster terrain" (page 4). This refocusing on "the essentials" means standards that are self-consciously set low but will create a situation in which "less is still more." To this end, they recommend a series of "filters" for examining and rejecting content that is not "essential," or that can be put off to later grades or indefinitely. Filter 6, for example, asks, "Is it truly necessary for college and work and thus should be provided for all, or an element of advanced math for only some students to pursue?"

If it is not "important for all," according to

their approach, it shouldn't be a standard. For a short period before the Common Core Mathematics Standards were finalized in 2010, the architects of the standards promised that they would develop supplemental standards for students who are willing and able to go beyond the very basic level embodied in the Common Core itself. They put in the "stubs" that were placeholders for more advanced concepts. This idea, however, was dropped in the final version of the Common Core. Thus Coleman and Zimba's 2007 vision of standards that set expectations at close to rock bottom so that they were easy enough for virtually everyone to achieve was realized in the version of the Common Core that became law in 46 states.

If our primary concern should be to boost the numbers of students who pass eighth-grade mathematics, then the Common Core could well be the ticket. If our primary concern should be to foster the intellectual achievement of all students to the highest

levels they are capable of attaining, then the Common Core is probably not the route forward.

Concern for the underdog is an admirable part of American thought and feeling. We don't serve the country very well by putting in place a system of standards that dooms the majority to failure. The key is to find a way to challenge everyone to do his best and to recognize and advance the challenges to those whose best is higher than average.

Back to that 2007 document. Coleman and Zimba wrote:

A fewer / clearer / higher approach should help our nation's students compete better once they enter the workforce. Instead of a weak recall of a vaster terrain, perhaps it is more effective to have true mastery of the essential parts of math and scientific thinking, so that our citizens will readily apply them to jobs we cannot even yet envision today.

"True mastery of the essential parts" is a nice way of saying, "Let's narrow our expecta-

tions." Is that truly in the nation's interests? I ask this not as a rhetorical question. If the essential part were learning how to use our lungs to breathe, that would be more important than trying to teach everyone the "vaster terrain" of singing opera, performing yoga, yodeling, and producing stage whispers. There are essentials that are really essential. I am not sure how to apply this to mathematics. Humans can get along pretty well with rudimentary mathematics, even in our complex, postindustrial society. *Essential* in this instance probably means learning to count and how to add and subtract with a calculator. Is that really what we want for the coming generations? *That* question is indeed rhetorical. We all want something higher than that. The real question is how much higher.

STANDARDS AND SECRETS

The argument I have presented against the Common Core has skirted many points that are prominent in the opposition. I have

avoided going into the details of the standards themselves mostly because to do so is tedious and unenlightening. The standards don't reveal themselves in narrow quotation. The Common Core State Standards for Reading Literature in Grade 3 include:

CCSS.ELA-LITERACY.RL.3.4 Determine the meaning of words and phrases as they are used in a text, distinguishing literal from non-literal language.

It and many statements like it are bland, uncontroversial declarations. To understand what the Common Core does to "reading" requires working through hundreds of these standards and seeing how they work together and relate to the larger project. It is a worthwhile exercise and, like several other critics of the Common Core, I've pursued it. But what really matters is the larger picture. When it comes to reading, the larger picture is that the Common Core puts a huge emphasis on teaching children to read for "informa-

tion." The other purposes of reading fade away. Reading is at its heart metaphoric. It teaches us to see things we otherwise couldn't or wouldn't. It schools our emotions; it points to truths beyond itself and, alternatively, it conveys lies; it may possess beauty or it may be ugly; it can cause us to ask questions that the text itself does not ask; it possesses implications; it belongs to and participates in a larger context; it taps into secret memories; and it rallies us to public causes.

The Common Core can't stop reading from doing that, but it can make all those things less likely for the average student. It does that by putting literature in modest quantities in the

---

The Common Core takes its origins in what President George W. Bush once called "the soft bigotry of low expectations."

---

primary grades and tapering it off until by the end of high school it is a negligible part of the curriculum. Poetry is especially hard-hit. The Common Core essentially puts imaginative literature on the far side of a hill and leaves students mostly with what the standards writers call "informational texts." Works of literature that have endured for generations (think of *Huckleberry Finn*) aren't banished entirely but fade into relative insignificance.

Worse, it presents most examples of important writing in the form of excerpts, and, still worse, it drastically plays down historical context. The infamous example that critics of the Common Core often cite is teaching the Gettysburg Address without explaining that it is a memorial speech over the most important battlefield of the Civil War.

There are many more such observations to be made about the substance of both the Mathematics and English Language Arts sections of the Common Core. But those criticisms are widely available elsewhere. Moreover, these are things that might, with

goodwill, be fixed. There are deeper problems with the Common Core that are probably beyond remedy.

SELF-POSSESSION

The Common Core was sold to America as a set of standards that would make students "college- and career-ready." That phrase is ubiquitous in Common Core writings. The emphasis really falls on the "college-ready" part, since the Common Core pays little attention to what will happen to students for whom a high school diploma is a terminal degree. But "college-ready" is itself something of a ruse. One way to make students ready for college is to provide a fairly demanding K-12 education that prepares them for the difficulties of real college courses. But there is another approach: persuade colleges to lower their standards.

The Common Core does a little of both. For some students, a Common Core curriculum that was taught by good teachers would

lift them to a higher level of performance than they currently receive in some of our not-so-ambitious and not-so-orderly classrooms. On the other hand, one of the conditions laid down in the Race to the Top was that the states had to agree to exempt students who finish Common Core-aligned high schools from having to take remedial courses in state colleges and universities. Since nearly half of students admitted to college in state universities in states like California are currently remanded to remedial courses, this no-remediation requirement will essentially force the colleges to lower their standards. The students will still take remedial courses, but those courses will be counted as the real thing.

This is a relatively minor point in the larger story of the Common Core, but it catches something deeper than itself. The Common Core is, in the end, a fake. Its proponents celebrate it as a great improvement in American schooling, but it is truly just a plaything for educrats, politicians, and ideologues.

When the framers of the Constitution left education to the states and localities, they made a fateful decision about what kind of nation we would become. We became a nation of restless experimenters, people with local loyalties as well as broader connections, people with only so much patience for education and what our betters had to say. It hasn't always worked out for the best. We make abundant mistakes as individuals and as communities. We do, however, have a capacity for self-correction, and we have pride in fixing what doesn't work.

The Common Core rubs against those virtues in an unpleasant way. The Common Core requires us to cede to others the diagnosis of where we have gone wrong and what we must do to set things right. That's demoralizing, pretty much to everyone except the handful of central planners who are in charge of the Common Core itself. *They* can be pretty happy as our überteachers, data wranglers, and custodians of social justice. The rest of us feel, well, *manipulated*.

The Common Core requires us to cede to others the diagnosis of where we have gone wrong and what we must do to set things right.

I don't celebrate local control of schools as a glorious thing. I've seen schools be run into the ground by inept local control. I've seen many other schools content in proud mediocrity. But state and local control can also ignite excellence, and I prefer the chances it offers of that to the dead certainty of the Common Core.

The Common Core came to us by means of deception. It grew up as a joint project of the deceivers and the deceived, including many of our elected leaders. That's an awfully unpromising start for reforming something as vital as America's schools. Just maybe the

basic premise is mistaken. We won't squeeze better educational "performance" from students by imposing a national regimen of standards and tests but will instead breed a deeper alienation and lassitude by taking away – or at least shrinking – the imaginative horizons of students, parents, teachers, and the communities in which they live.

What is truly common and at the core of American life is our sense of freedom and self-governance. The Common Core is at war with those ideals.